Make your own Silk Flowers

By DEE ENTREKIN

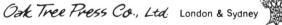

STERLING PUBLISHING CO., INC. NEW YORK

Oak Tree Press Co., Ltd. London & Sydney

Contents

Copyright © 1975 by Sterling Publishing Co., Inc.
Two Park Avenue, New York, N.Y. 10016
Distributed in Australia by Oak Tree Press Co., Ltd.,
P.O. Box J34, Brickfield Hill, Sydney 2000, N.S.W.
Distributed in the United Kingdom
by Ward Lock Ltd., 116 Baker Street, London W 1
Manufactured in the United States of America
All rights reserved
Library of Congress Catalog Card No.: 74–31705
Sterling ISBN 0–8069–5318–7 Trade   Oak Tree 7061–2077–9
           5319–5 Library   2788–9 Paper
           8994–7 Paper

ACKNOWLEDGMENTS

The author would like to express her appreciation to Mrs. John G. McReynolds who created the flower arrangements and who has shared her knowledge of arranging flowers with countless numbers of people for the past 50 years. The author is particularly indebted to Mrs. Eugene B. Bruton who, being unfamiliar with making silk flowers, read the manuscript for clarification, and to Miss Barbara Shores who assisted with the drawings. The photography was done by Charles W. Pittman and Fred M. Muncher.

Illus. 1. A lovely arrangement of garden flowers will enhance any area you wish to decorate.

Introduction

Artists and crafters have always strived to imitate the natural perfection and brilliance of flowers—on canvas, with oil or water colors, as well as from paper and cloth of all types—colored construction paper, tissue paper, crepe paper, cottons and silk, for instance. Magnificent handmade silk flowers have even begun to fill the gift and decorating shops, but for quite high prices.

The aim of this book is to teach you how to make your own silk flowers, so you can decorate your home with stunningly natural-looking flowers for a fraction of what it would cost you to buy them.

The flowers only appear to be complicated to make. The techniques are simple and you should be successful with your first creations. If you simply follow the steps set forth here, you can capture in silk the natural beauty of real flowers.

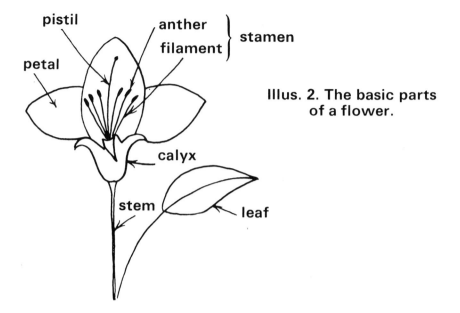

Illus. 2. The basic parts of a flower.

Basic Parts of a Flower

The flowers in this book have been simplified as much as possible without altering their appearance. It is helpful, however, to know the basic parts of a flower. Study Illus. 2 and 3 as well as real flowers.

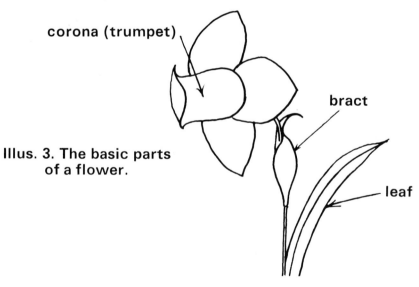

Illus. 3. The basic parts of a flower.

Supplies and Equipment

Read through the general instructions beginning on page 10 before gathering the supplies and equipment to make silk flowers. Understanding their uses will enable you to acquire the various materials in the amounts you need. Some of the supplies are necessary to make all the flowers, while others are used for specific flowers only.

You need:

China silk (see page 78)
cornstarch
household paint brush, 1 to $1\frac{1}{2}$ inches (25 to 37.5 mm.) wide
sponge or washcloth
cardboard, shirt-type (not very heavy)
pencil
scissors
waxed paper
paper towels
felt-tip markers, permanent and thick-lined
white cotton-covered wire, size 30
green cotton-covered wire, size 30
green cotton-covered wire, size 24
stem wire, gauge #16, or coat hanger wire
white glue, clear and quick drying
wire cutters
small jar, with lid
small artist's paint brush
cotton balls
Styrofoam (plastic foam)
light green floral tape
pinking shears

**Illus. 4. Glorious bursts of color stand out beauti-
fully against a brick wall.**

spool wire or strong thread
charcoal pencil or black fine-line felt-tip marker
yellow chenille stems
soft pastels
clear acrylic spray or fixative

Keep the supplies together in a box or flat basket. Smaller
boxes are useful for storing patterns, stamens, petals, felt-tip
markers, and other items. Wash your brushes with soap and

water before putting them away. Place the cap on the jar containing the diluted glue after each use. Press wrinkles out of the fabric before you size it.

As your skill develops, you may need other supplies and equipment to aid you in making numerous other flowers. These will be mentioned throughout the text.

To clean your silk flowers, dust them periodically with a small feather duster.

Fabrics

China Silk

China silk is a thin, pure silk that is primarily used for lining handmade sweaters and other garments. Shops specializing in fine fabrics usually stock white, black, and a limited variety of other colors. China silk is also available from mail-order companies specializing in imported silks.

Other Fabrics

You can use rayon or rayon and silk blends if they do not have special or protective finishes. Other synthetic fabrics cannot be used satisfactorily with the method described here for making silk flowers. If you select a fabric other than China silk, the following test should be made: Cut diagonally through a scrap of the fabric in question. Following the instructions outlined under *Finishing the Petal and Leaf Edges* (see page 14), paint the diagonally cut edge with diluted glue and roll it. If the roll stays in place, you can proceed with the fabric chosen.

It is possible to make flowers from almost any kind of fabric by omitting the instructions for finishing the edges. After you have sized the fabric (explained under *Sizing the Fabric*, page 10), the edges will not fray unduly and the resulting flower will be quite beautiful. However, this procedure involves a more complicated technique of shaping the flowers than outlined in the following instructions. Once you are skilled in these procedures, you may wish to try other materials. The guidelines set forth under *Increasing the Varieties of Flowers* on page 76 will be helpful.

General Instructions

The following instructions explain the basic procedures for making silk flowers. Individual variations and more specific details are contained in the following chapters.

Patterns

The patterns included in this book were developed by studying and copying real flowers. (This is discussed in detail under *Making Medium- or Large-Petalled Flowers*.) They are included as guidelines for you to follow and hopefully will suggest other flowers that you can make in a similar manner.

It is sometimes necessary to alter the actual shape of a petal or the middle of a flower to simplify the process of making it. The rose pattern is a good example. An actual rose petal is not shaped like the pattern given and it has many more petals than the 11 called for. However, the pattern and directions given produce a beautiful rose that is easy to make.

To begin, draw the pattern for the flower you are making onto cardboard according to the diagrams. One square on the graph equals one inch. To enlarge a pattern, draw criss-cross lines vertically and horizontally, spaced one inch apart, on paper. Copy the pattern one square at a time and transfer the pattern onto cardboard. Label each pattern piece with all necessary information.

Sizing the Fabric

A starch is applied to the silk or other fabric before you do anything else for several reasons: it adds body, makes the fabric easier to handle, softens the sheen of the silk, and protects against the absorption of dust.

To make the sizing, mix one tablespoon (15 ml.) of cornstarch

Illus. 5. Brush the sizing onto the silk as shown here.

with one tablespoon (15 ml.) of water in a small cup. Measure $\frac{7}{8}$ cup (210 ml.) of water, place in a small container, and bring to a boil. Remove the boiling water from the heat and slowly add the cornstarch and water mixture, stirring constantly. (Make sure the mixture of cornstarch and water is well blended before adding it to the boiling water.) Add one tablespoon (15 ml.) of white clear-drying glue and mix thoroughly. Cover and let cool. The sizing is then ready to be applied to the silk.

Use a small household brush, about an inch (25 mm.) wide, or a soft, smooth sponge to apply the solution. Some craft shops stock a handled sponge that is ideal for this purpose. Lay the silk, right side up, on a clean, plastic-laminated or glass surface. For best results, work with small pieces of silk, preferably not larger than 12 × 18 inches (30 × 45 cm.). Take care to keep the silk smooth and the grain of the fabric straight. Brush the sizing onto the silk as shown in Illus. 5.

After you have applied the sizing to the silk, remove the excess with a soft, dampened washcloth or sponge (see Illus. 6).

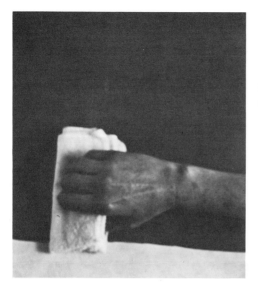

Illus. 6. Remove any excess sizing with a soft, dampened washcloth or sponge.

Wipe over the surface, working out any wrinkles or air bubbles that may have formed. Rinse out the sponge and continue to wipe the surface until the silk is smooth and there are no traces of excess starch remaining. As the silk dries, it adheres to the surface that it has been placed on. When thoroughly dry, loosen one edge of the silk and carefully pull the fabric up (see Illus. 7). The side of the silk that was placed next to

Illus. 7. When the silk is completely dry, loosen one edge and carefully pull the fabric up.

the plastic or glass surface is slick and glossy. Keep this in mind when assembling the flowers. Use the glossy side of the fabric for the underside of the petals and leaves or that side of the petals that is least visible. (The white glue used in the sizing is water soluble, so you can easily clean the work surface with warm water and detergent.)

Work Area

Work close to a sink so that you can keep your hands clean at all times. Protect the surface of the work table with a piece of waxed paper or plastic. Lay several paper towels on top of the waxed paper. When the top paper towel becomes dirty, remove it. Always work on clean paper towels. Have wet towels close by to wipe glue from your hands.

Coloring the Silk

It is best to work with silk that is similar in color to the flower being made. If this is not available, you can color white fabric with thick-lined felt-tip markers after you have sized the silk. These markers are readily available at variety stores but usually only in the primary and intermediate colors. School and office supply or art supply shops generally stock a large range of shades and tints in the permanent markers.

Before coloring the silk, protect the surface of the work table as described under *Work Area* above.

Size the silk before you color it with permanent felt-tip markers. Even though the markers are considered waterproof, the color is likely to bleed when wet. If you size it after you have colored it, the sizing could cause the color to streak, ruining the silk and the work surface.

Lay the sized silk out and, using the pattern for the flower, estimate how much silk you will need. Cut off the required amount and lay it on top of the paper towels. Now color the silk with the marker. Draw the marker slowly over the silk in one direction, as shown in Illus. 8, until you have colored the entire piece. The silk absorbs the color evenly and dries quickly.

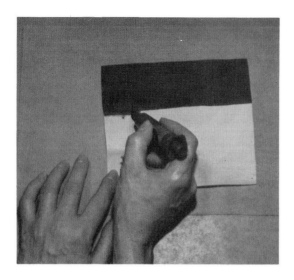

Illus. 8. To color silk after it has been sized, draw a thick-lined felt-tip marker slowly over the silk in one direction.

Distinct markings on flowers such as pansies or poppies are also applied with markers. These markings are not applied until later on in the development of the flowers and are explained where applicable.

Cutting Out the Fabric

The arrows on each pattern indicate the grain line markings. Place the pattern on the fabric with the grain line marking running parallel to the selvage. Draw around the pattern with a sharp pencil and cut out the fabric flower part. Be sure to cut away all the pencil markings.

Mixing the Glue

Mix 2 tablespoons (30 ml.) of glue with 2 tablespoons (30 ml.) of water in a small jar. Use this diluted glue when finishing the petal and leaf edges and making stamens.

Finishing the Petal and Leaf Edges

Place a silk petal on a paper towel. Dip a small artist's brush into the diluted glue and paint around the edge of the petal. Steady your hand by resting your wrist on the table so that you can apply the glue solution smoothly, creating an $\frac{1}{8}$ inch- (3.18 mm.-) wide stroke around the outer edge

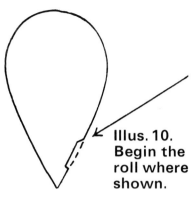

Illus. 10. Begin the roll where shown.

Illus. 9. Paint diluted glue around the outer edge.

(Illus. 9). Now roll the edge of the petal towards the middle using the thumb and forefinger of your right hand. Begin the roll about ½ inch (12.7 mm.) from the bottom of the right side of the petal (Illus. 10). While holding the petal with your left hand, place the petal's edge flatly between your thumb and forefinger, and force your thumb forward. This causes the edge to roll (Illus. 11).

After you have started the roll, finish the lower ½ inch (12.7 mm.) by using your left thumb and forefinger and reversing the procedure. Finish rolling the raw edge, holding the petal taut by pulling back with your left hand while rolling forward

Illus. 11. Holding the petal in your left hand, place the petal's edge between your thumb and forefinger, and force your thumb forward, thus causing the edge to roll.

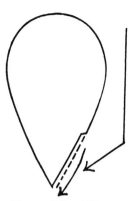

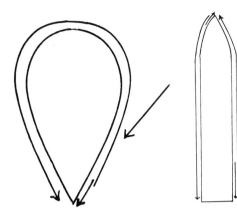

Illus. 12. After you have started the roll, finish the lower ½ inch using your left thumb and forefinger.

Illus. 13. Now roll completely around the raw edge of the petal or leaf.

Illus. 14. When the tops are pointed, roll one side, turn, and then begin the roll again on the other side.

with your right hand (Illus. 13). (Finish the edges of the leaves in the same way.)

When the tops of the petals and leaves are pointed, finish one side, then turn the piece and roll down the other side (Illus. 14). Do not roll the straight bottom edges of the long leaves or petals. The roll will be on the top of the petal or leaf.

NOTE: If you are left-handed, reverse the instructions and begin the roll on the left side of the petal or leaf. Practice.

Many of the petals and leaves are cut on the bias of the silk. When finishing the edges, the fabric will tend to stretch out of shape. Do not be concerned about this. After the edges are finished, re-shape the petals or leaves into their original forms. The rippling effect created by the roll adds to the natural appearance of the finished flower.

Shading the Petals

Vivid or subtle variations of color are characteristic of many flowers. You can produce the most realistic results by having the actual flowers to copy. When this is not possible, use large, clear color pictures instead. Bulb and seed catalogues are excellent for this purpose.

Add the shading after you have finished the edges of the petals. It would seem logical to shade the flat petals first, but the pastels prevent the glue from holding the rolled edges in place.

Use soft pastels, found in art supply shops, on the top side of the petals to do the shading. Do not add shading to the backs of the petals because then the glue would not be effective holding the support wires. After applying the pastels, use a cotton ball or small clean brush to blend the colors. Use the pastels sparingly, adding more if necessary.

Spray the shading with a clear acrylic spray or fixative to set the shading *after* attaching the support wires or after you have assembled the flower, because the fixative weakens the holding power of the glue. Hold the can at least 2 feet (60 cm.) away from the flower. Use the spray in a well ventilated area.

A good example of shading is found under the instructions for the day lily on page 49.

Illus. 15. Once you have made your silk flowers, try to arrange them artistically.

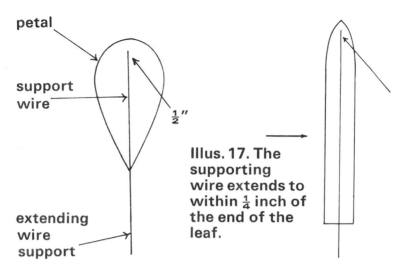

petal

support wire

$\frac{1}{2}''$

extending wire support

Illus. 17. The supporting wire extends to within ¼ inch of the end of the leaf.

Illus. 16. Glue a supporting wire to the back of the petals and leaves.

Petal and Leaf Supports

Use cotton-covered wires, available in white or green and in various sizes, to support the petals and leaves. As the name implies, the wires are covered with a cotton thread wound tightly round the wire. They are stocked by most craft shops and can be ordered from craft catalogues.

Glue the cotton-covered wire to the middle of the back of each petal and leaf. (The petals of roses and sweet peas are not wired.) The small white cotton-covered wires (size 30) support the petals. Use a felt-tip marker to color the wires to match the petals. Small green wires (size 30) support the short leaves. Large green wires (size 24) support the long leaves.

The supporting wires extend beyond the bottoms of the petals and leaves for easier assembly (Illus. 16). The exact length of the wires varies according to the size of the petals and leaves. Measure the length of the petals or leaves and add 2 inches (50 mm.) to determine how long to cut the wire. Allow more than 2 inches (50 mm.) for short leaves so the extending wires can serve as stems.

Apply full-strength glue sparingly to one end of the wire

and glue it to the middle of the back of the petal or leaf. Be sure the roll of the petal or leaf is on the top side, and the supporting wire is on the bottom side. The supporting wire for a petal should end about ½ inch (12.7 mm.) from the top of the petal (Illus. 16). The supporting wire for a leaf should end about ¼ inch (6.35 mm.) from the end of the leaf (Illus. 17). After you have attached the wires, place the pieces in Styrofoam (plastic foam) to dry.

Making the Stamens

The size of the stamens depends upon the kind of flower being made. Make the stamens for daffodils, irises, crocuses, and pansies as follows: Cut a length of small white cotton-covered wire about 4 inches (100 mm.) long for each stamen (Illus. 18). Pinch off a small flat piece of cotton that is about ¼ inch (6.35 mm.) in diameter. Moisten the piece of cotton with diluted glue and place it on top of one end of the cotton-covered wire (Illus. 19). Twist the cotton to form an oval shape (Illus. 20). Place each stamen in plastic foam to dry. When dry, color the stamens with felt-tip markers.

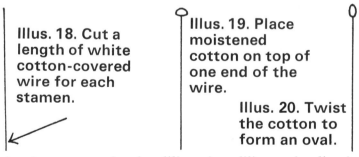

Illus. 18. Cut a length of white cotton-covered wire for each stamen.

Illus. 19. Place moistened cotton on top of one end of the wire.

Illus. 20. Twist the cotton to form an oval.

Make the stamens for day lilies, tiger lilies and tulips in the same way, but with these changes: Cut the wires 5 to 6 inches (125 to 150 mm.) long for day lilies and tiger lilies. Cut the wires about 4 inches (100 mm.) long for tulips. Double the size of the pieces of cotton used to make the anthers (heads) of the stamens.

The number of stamens required for each of the different kinds of flowers is given under the instructions for the individual flowers.

Assembling the Flowers and Leaves

The assembly of the flowers and leaves is covered under the instructions for the individual flowers. Generally, you put the flowers together by placing the petals round the middles, keeping the bottoms of the petals even. Assemble and attach the leaves after you add the main stems. Before attaching long leaves, apply glue to the bottom raw edges and wrap loosely round the main stems before wrapping with floral tape. This produces a more natural appearance of growth.

Attaching the Stems

Attach the stems after you have assembled the flowers and leaves. Place the wire, usually a #16 gauge wire or wire from a coat hanger, close to the base of the flower and next to the extending wire supports (Illus. 21). Then wrap the wires tightly together with light green floral tape. Wrap the tape down the length of the stem wire. Attach the leaves to the stems with additional floral tape (Illus. 22). Leave the stems long until you arrange the flowers.

Illus. 22 (right). Wrap the extending wires and stem wire together with floral tape. As you wrap down the stem, attach the leaves.

Illus. 21 (left). Place the stem wire next to the extending wire supports.

It is assumed throughout the rest of the book that you have a thorough understanding of these basic instructions, and that you will refer to them as you proceed to make the following flowers. After making these flowers, you should have no difficulty developing others using the techniques you have learned.

Tulip

Illus. 23. Create a perpetual springtime by making colorful silk tulips.

To begin, size and color your fabric as described in the general instructions. The suggested colors for tulips are: white, yellow, orange, pink, red, and purple for the petals and green for the leaves. Then, using the tulip pattern in Illus. 24 and following Illus. 25, cut out six petals and one leaf for each

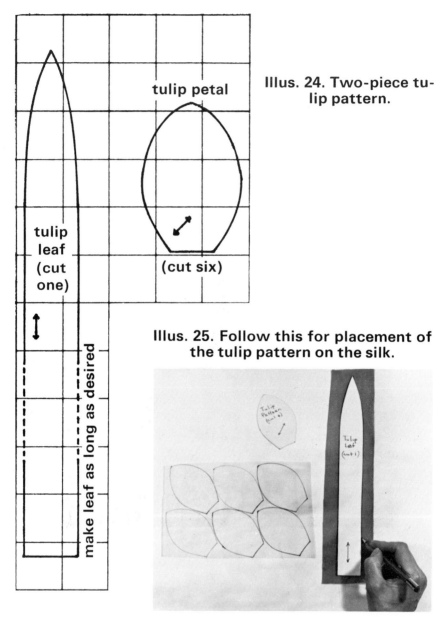

tulip petal

tulip leaf (cut one)

(cut six)

make leaf as long as desired

Illus. 24. Two-piece tulip pattern.

Illus. 25. Follow this for placement of the tulip pattern on the silk.

flower you wish to make. Next, roll the edges of the petals and the leaf (Illus. 11). Set these aside.

Cut six pieces of white cotton-covered wire, each about 5 inches (125 mm.) long, for petal supports (Illus. 16). Using a felt-tip marker, color the wires to match the petals. Then,

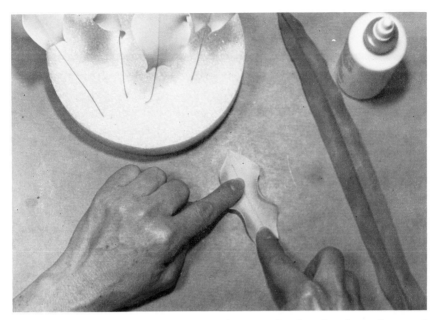

Illus. 26. Glue a supporting wire to the back of each petal.

using full-strength glue sparingly, glue a supporting wire to the middle of the back of each petal (Illus. 26). Stick the petals in plastic foam to dry.

Cut a piece of heavy green cotton-covered wire (the length of the leaf plus 2 inches or 50 mm.) for the leaf support. Glue the supporting wire to the middle of the back of the leaf (Illus. 26). Stick the leaf in plastic foam to dry.

Make six stamens and stick in plastic foam to dry. Then,

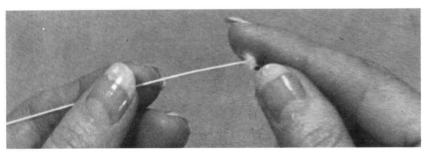

Illus. 27. Make a stamen by first glueing a small piece of cotton to the end of a length of cotton-covered wire and then shaping the cotton into an oval.

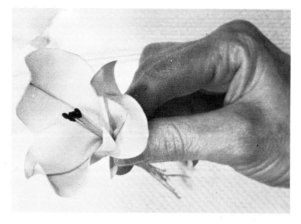

Illus. 28. Space three petals evenly round the stamens as shown.

color the filaments (stems) yellow, and the anthers (heads) brown.

Assembling the Tulip

Begin assembling the tulip with the six stamens. The tops of the stamens should be even. Hold the stamens together with a short piece of floral tape, attached about $1\frac{1}{2}$ inches (37.5 mm.) down from the tops of the stamens. Apply a small amount of glue across the inside bottom of each petal, then space three petals evenly round the stamens (Illus. 28). The petals will curve upwards, so be sure the right side of each petal is facing outward. The glue holds the petals in place. The stamens should extend at least an inch (25 mm.) above the base of the petals.

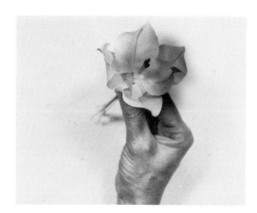

Illus. 29. Place the remaining three petals around and between the first three.

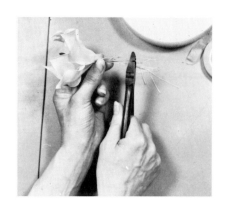

Illus. 30. Cut the extending wire supports different lengths to eliminate bulk.

Place the remaining three petals around and between the first three petals (Illus. 29). Always keep the bottoms of the petals even. Cut the extending wire supports different lengths to eliminate bulk (Illus. 30). Attach a stem wire to the extending wire supports with floral tape. Wrap the floral tape down the stem. Then attach the leaf about two-thirds of the way down with additional tape. Shape the tulip by rounding the petals upwards.

Your first silk flower is complete.

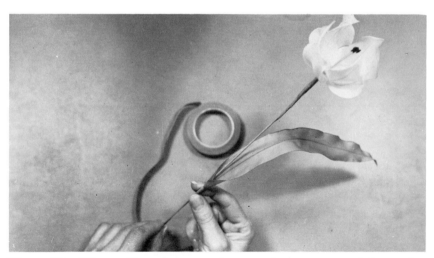

Illus. 31. Wrap floral tape down the stem, adding the leaf about two-thirds of the way down, as shown.

Daffodil

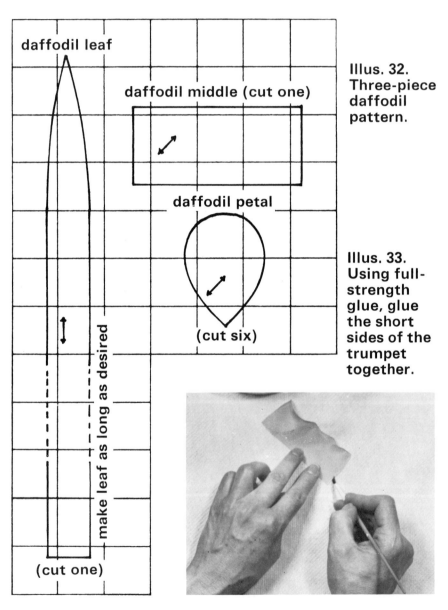

daffodil leaf

daffodil middle (cut one)

daffodil petal

(cut six)

make leaf as long as desired

(cut one)

Illus. 32. Three-piece daffodil pattern.

Illus. 33. Using full-strength glue, glue the short sides of the trumpet together.

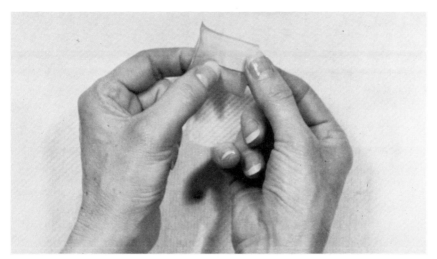

Illus. 34. Form a cylinder, making sure the rolled edge is on the outside.

The suggested colors for daffodils are: white and yellow for the petals, yellow, orange, white, and apricot for the trumpets and green for the leaves.

Using the three-piece daffodil pattern in Illus. 32, cut out six petals, one trumpet (the cylindrical part in the middle of the petals), and one leaf for each flower.

Roll the edges of the petals and the leaf and then roll one long edge of the trumpet. Cut six pieces of white cotton-covered wire, each about 5 inches (125 mm.) long, for petal supports. Using a felt-tip marker, color the wires to match the petals.

Using full-strength glue sparingly, glue a supporting wire to the middle of the back of each petal. Stick the petals in plastic foam to dry. Cut a piece of heavy green cotton-covered wire (the length of the leaf plus 2 inches or 50 mm.) for the leaf support. Glue the supporting wire to the middle of the back of the leaf. Stick the leaf in plastic foam to dry.

Using full-strength glue, glue the short sides of the trumpet together to form a cylinder, making sure the roll is on the outside of the cylinder (Illus. 33 and 34). Make six small stamens and stick in plastic foam to dry. Then color the stamens yellow with a felt-tip marker.

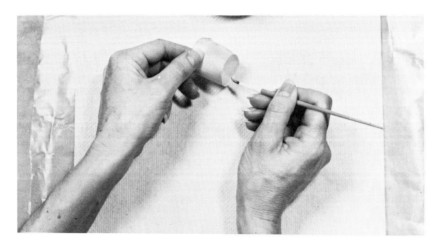

Illus. 35. Apply a bit of full-strength glue round the inside bottom of the trumpet before adding the stamens.

Assembling the Daffodil

Begin assembling the daffodil with the six stamens. The tops of the stamens should be even. Hold the stamens together with a short piece of floral tape, attached about $1\frac{1}{2}$ inches (37.5 mm.) below the tops of the stamens. Apply a small amount of full-strength glue round the inside bottom of the trumpet (Illus. 35). (The unrolled edge is the bottom.) Hold the stamens inside the trumpet (Illus. 36). Gather the bottom edge

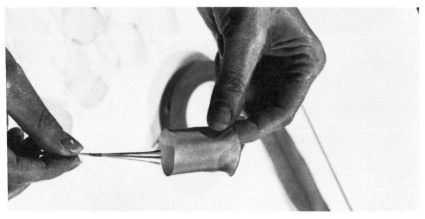

Illus. 36. Hold the stamens inside the trumpet.

Illus. 37 (above). A single yellow daffodil looks elegant in any pretty vase.

Illus. 38 (left). You will think it is spring all year round if you make a lovely bouquet of silk daffodils to set upon a table.

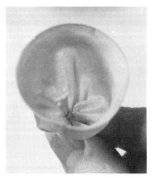

Illus. 39. Gather the bottom edge of the trumpet evenly around the stamens.

Illus. 40. Space three petals evenly around the trumpet. Hold in place with floral tape.

Illus. 41. Place the remaining three petals around and between the first three. Hold them in place with floral tape.

Illus. 42. Cut the extending wire supports different lengths to eliminate bulk.

evenly round the stamens (Illus. 39). The glue holds the bottom in place. The stamens should extend about an inch (25 mm.) above the base of the trumpet.

Space three petals evenly round the trumpet (Illus. 40). Keep the bottoms of the petals even with the bottom of the trumpet. Hold the petals in place with a short piece of floral tape wrapped below the petals. Place the remaining three petals around and between the first three petals (Illus. 41). Hold these petals in place with a short piece of tape. Cut the extending wire supports different lengths to eliminate bulk (Illus. 42). Attach a stem wire to the extending wire supports with floral tape. Wrap the tape down the stem (Illus. 43). Then attach the leaf about two-thirds of the way down with additional tape (Illus. 44). Shape the daffodil by curving the petals outwards. Bend the neck of the stem so the finished flower faces forward rather than upward.

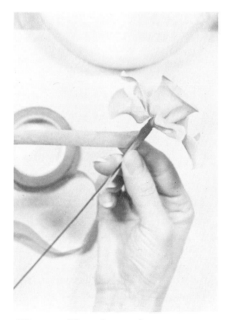

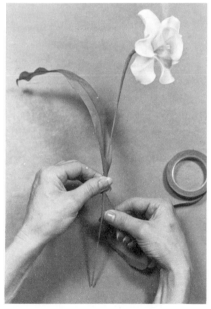

Illus. 43. Attach a stem wire, next to the cut extending wire supports, with floral tape.

Illus. 44. Attach the leaf about two-thirds the way down the stem, using additional floral tape.

Poppy

Illus. 45. Magnificent red poppies add a cheerful splash of color to an otherwise dark corner.

The suggested colors for poppies are: red, yellow, and pink for the petals, black for the middles and green for the leaves.

Using the poppy pattern in Illus. 46, cut out six petals, one middle, and one leaf for each flower.

Cut the long edges of the flower's middle with pinking shears. Clip between the points of the pinked edges about $\frac{1}{2}$ inch

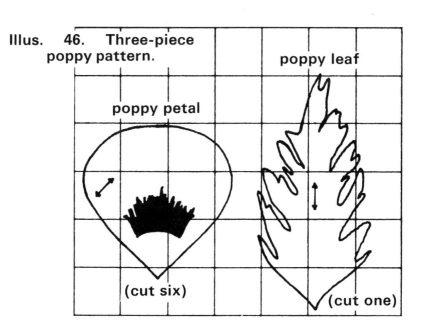

Illus. 46. Three-piece poppy pattern.

poppy leaf

poppy petal

(cut six)

(cut one)

gather between dotted lines

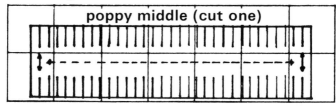

poppy middle (cut one)

clip ½ inch deep

(12.7 mm.) deep as indicated on the pattern, and as shown in Illus. 47. Cut a piece of white cotton-covered wire 6 inches (150 mm.) long. Color the wire with a black felt-tip marker.

Illus. 47. Clip between the points on the poppy's middle about ½ inch deep.

33

Illus. 48. Gather the poppy's center through the middle.

Illus. 49. Loop the wire round the gathered center, with the clipped edges pointing upwards.

Gather the flower center through the middle (Illus. 48). Loop the wire round the gathered center, having the clipped edges pointing upward (Illus. 49). Twist the wire to hold the gathers in place (Illus. 50) and set aside.

Color the shaded area of the petals with a black felt-tip marker where shown on the pattern (see also Illus. 51). Roll the edges of the petals and let dry. Cut six pieces of white cotton-covered wire, each about 5 inches (125 mm.) long, for petal supports. Using a felt-tip marker, color the wires to match the petals.

Illus. 50. Twist the wire to hold the gathers in place.

Illus. 51. Color the shaded areas of the poppy pattern with a black felt-tip marker where shown.

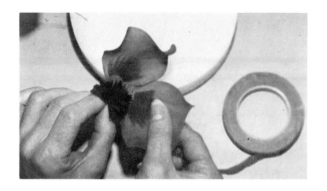

Illus. 52. Begin assembling the poppy by adding three petals evenly round the middle.

Glue a supporting wire to the middle of the back of each petal. Stick the petals in plastic foam to dry.

Cut a piece of small green cotton-covered wire about 5 inches (125 mm.) long for the leaf support. Glue the supporting wire to the middle of the back of the leaf. Stick the leaf in plastic foam to dry.

Assembling the Poppy

Begin assembling the poppy by adding three of the petals evenly round the middle, keeping the base of the petals even (Illus. 52). Hold the petals in place with a short piece of floral tape wrapped below the petals. Add the remaining three petals round and between the first three petals. Hold these in place with tape (Illus. 53).

Illus. 53. Add the remaining three petals round and between the first three. Hold them in place with floral tape.

35

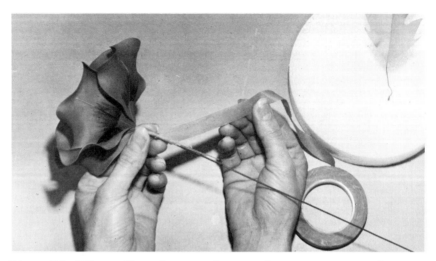

Illus. 54. Wrap floral tape down the stem over the extending wire supports which you have cut to different lengths to eliminate bulk.

Cut the extending wire supports different lengths to eliminate bulk. Attach a stem wire to the extending wire supports with floral tape. Wrap the tape down the stem (Illus. 54). Then attach the leaf about 4 inches (100 mm.) below the flower with additional tape (Illus. 55). Shape the finished poppy by cupping the petals upwards.

Illus. 55. Attach the leaf about 4 inches below the flower with additional floral tape.

Peony

The suggested colors for peonies are: white and pale pink to deep fuchsia for the petals, yellow for the middles and green for the leaves.

Illus. 56. Silk peonies look so real that you will probably even try to smell them yourself!

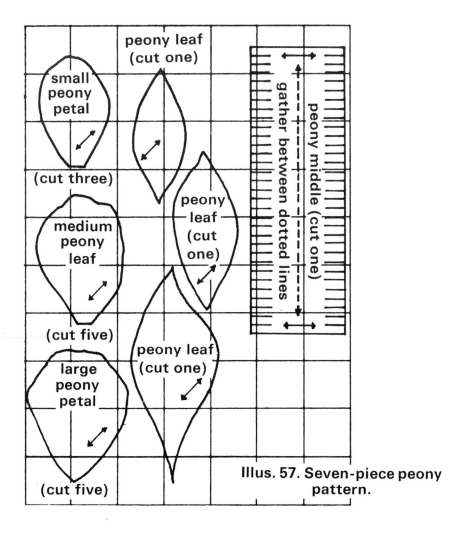

small peony petal

(cut three)

peony leaf (cut one)

medium peony leaf

peony leaf (cut one)

(cut five)

large peony petal

peony leaf (cut one)

(cut five)

gather between dotted lines

peony middle (cut one)

Illus. 57. Seven-piece peony pattern.

Using the peony pattern in Illus. 57, cut out three small petals, five medium petals, and five large petals for each flower. Cut out one middle for each flower. Cut out one of each leaf for each flower.

Cut the long edges of the flower's middle with pinking shears. Clip between the points of the pinked edges about $\frac{1}{2}$ inch (12.7 mm.) deep as indicated on the pattern. Cut a piece of white cotton-covered wire 6 inches (150 mm.) long. Color the wire with a yellow felt-tip marker. Gather the flower

Illus. 58. Gather the center of the peony through the middle.

Illus. 59. Loop the wire round the center.

Illus. 60. Twist the wire tightly to hold the gathers in place.

center through the middle (Illus. 58). Loop the wire round the center, having the clipped edges pointing upward (Illus. 59). Twist the wire to hold the gathers in place (Illus. 60) and set aside. Roll the petal and leaf edges and set aside.

Cut 13 pieces of white cotton-covered wire, each about 5 inches (125 mm.) long, for petal supports. Using a felt-tip marker, color the wires to match the petals. Glue a supporting wire to the middle of the back of each petal. Stick the petals in plastic foam to dry.

Cut three pieces of small green cotton-covered wire, each about 5 inches (125 mm.) long, for leaf supports. Glue a supporting wire to the middle of the back of each leaf. Stick the leaves in plastic foam to dry. When dry, place the three leaves together with one leaf extending about an inch (25 mm.) higher than the other two. Wrap the stems together with floral tape, beginning about an inch (25 mm.) below the two lower leaves (Illus. 61). Spread the two lower leaves outwards.

Illus. 61. How to wrap the stems together.

Illus. 62. First hold
the three small
petals in place,
half way round the
middle, with floral
tape.

Assembling the Peony

Begin assembling the peony by adding the three small petals half way round the yellow middle. Hold the petals in place with a short piece of floral tape wrapped below the petals (Illus. 62). Always keep the base of the petals even.

Add the five medium petals evenly round the middle. Hold these petals in place with floral tape. Then add the five large

Illus. 63. Add the five
medium petals even-
ly round the middle.

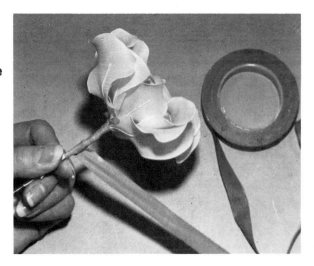

Illus. 64. Add the five large petals round and between the medium ones.

petals round and between the medium petals. Hold them in place with tape (Illus. 64).

Cut the extending wire supports different lengths to eliminate bulk. Attach a stem wire to the extending wire supports with tape. Wrap the floral tape down the stem. Then attach the leaves 3 or 4 inches (75 or 100 mm.) below the flower with additional tape (Illus. 65). Shape the finished flower by cupping the petals outwards and then upwards.

Illus. 65. Attach the leaves about 3 or 4 inches below the flower using floral tape.

Pansy

The suggested colors for pansies are: yellow, lavender, and deep purple for the petals and green for the leaves.

Using the pansy pattern in Illus. 66, cut out one of petal A, two of petal B, and two of petal C for each flower. Cut out one leaf for each flower.

Make the pansy markings on the petal marked A and the two petals marked B with a brown, purple, or black felt-tip marker, as shown on the pattern and in Illus. 67. Roll the petal and leaf edges and set aside.

Cut five pieces of white cotton-covered wire, each about

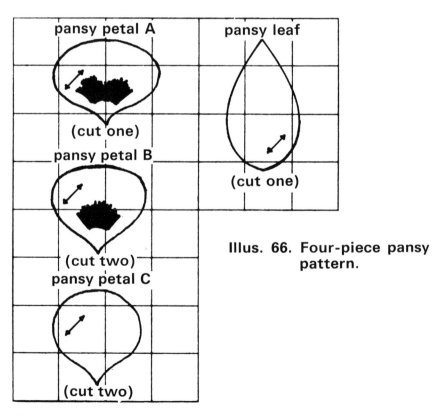

pansy petal A

(cut one)

pansy petal B

(cut two)

pansy petal C

(cut two)

pansy leaf

(cut one)

Illus. 66. Four-piece pansy pattern.

Illus. 67. Make the pansy markings with a felt-tip marker as shown.

4 inches (100 mm.) long, for petal supports. With a felt-tip marker, color the wires to match the petals. Glue a supporting wire to the middle of the back of each petal. Stick the petals in plastic foam to dry.

Cut a piece of small green cotton-covered wire 4 inches (100 mm.) long for the leaf support. Glue the wire to the middle of the back of the leaf. Stick the leaf in plastic foam to dry.

Make one small stamen and let it dry. Then, color it with a yellow felt-tip marker.

Assembling the Pansy

Begin assembling the pansy with the petal marked A. Turn petal A perpendicular to its stem, as shown in Illus. 68. Center the stamen at the bottom of petal A so that only the top of the stamen will be visible after you have completed the pansy. Hold the stamen in place with a short piece of floral tape (Illus. 69). Add the two petals marked B, towards the back

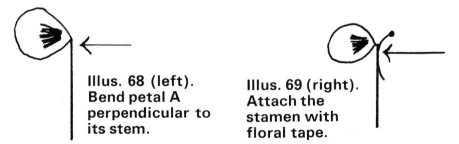

Illus. 68 (left). Bend petal A perpendicular to its stem.

Illus. 69 (right). Attach the stamen with floral tape.

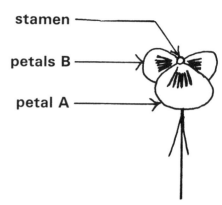

Illus. 70. Add the two petals marked B as shown.

Illus. 71. Diagram of positions for the petals marked B.

and slightly under each side of petal A, as shown in Illus. 70 and 71. Turn these petals up slightly. Hold them in place with tape wrapped below the petals.

Add the two petals marked C in back of the petals marked B (Illus. 72 and 73). These two petals should overlap slightly. Turn them back in the opposite direction of the petal marked A. Hold them in place with tape. Always keep the bottoms of the petals even when assembling the flowers.

Illus. 73. Close-up of where to add petals C.

Illus. 72. Add petals C.

Illus. 74. An arrangement of differently colored pansies is a pleasure to look at.

Cut the extending wire supports different lengths to eliminate bulk. Attach a stem wire to the extending wire supports with floral tape. Wrap the tape down the stem. Remember to attach the leaf about 3 inches (75 mm.) below the flower with additional tape (Illus. 75). Shape the pansy as described above.

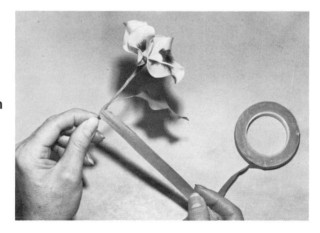

Illus. 75. Attach the pansy leaf about 3 inches below the flower.

Crocus

The suggested colors for crocuses are: white, yellow, lavender, blue, and purple for the petals and green for the leaves.

Using the crocus pattern in Illus. 76, cut out six petals and one leaf for each flower.

Roll the edges of the petals and the leaf. Cut six pieces of white cotton-covered wire, each about 4 inches (100 mm.)

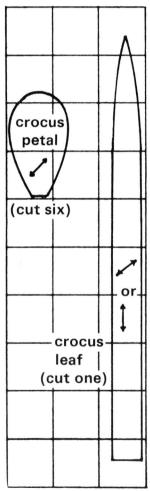

Illus. 76. Two-piece crocus pattern.

Illus. 77 (below). Space three petals evenly round the stamens, making sure that the petals curve upwards and outwards as shown.

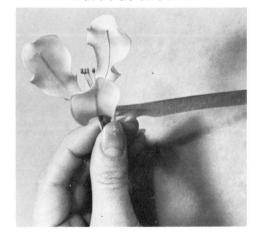

Illus. 78. Cut the wire supports and then attach a stem with floral tape.

long, for petal supports. Using a felt-tip marker, color the wires to match the petals. Glue a supporting wire to the middle of the back of each petal. Stick the petals in plastic foam to dry.

Cut one piece of heavy green cotton-covered wire (the length of the leaf plus 2 inches or 50 mm.) for the leaf support. Glue the wire to the middle of the back of the leaf. Stick the leaf in plastic foam to dry.

Make six small stamens and stick them in plastic foam to dry. Using a felt-tip marker, color the filaments (stems) yellow and the anthers (heads) orange.

Assembling the Crocus

Begin assembling the crocus with the six stamens. The tops of the stamens should be even. Hold the stamens together with a short piece of floral tape, attached about $1\frac{1}{2}$ inches (37.5 mm.) down from the top of the stamens. Space three of the petals evenly round the stamens. The petals curve upwards, so be sure the right sides of the petals are facing outwards (see Illus. 77). The stamens should extend about $\frac{5}{8}$ inch (16 mm.) above the base of the petals. Hold the petals in place with a short piece of floral tape wrapped below the petals.

Place the remaining three petals around and between the first three petals. Hold them in place with tape. Always keep the bottoms of the petals even. Cut the extending wire supports different lengths to eliminate bulk.

Attach a stem wire to the extending wire supports with floral tape. Wrap the tape down the stem (Illus. 78). Then attach the

Illus. 79. Make a permanent bunch of crocuses to enhance your décor.

leaf about two-thirds of the way down with additional tape (Illus. 80). Shape the finished crocus by rounding the petals upwards.

Illus. 80. Attach a leaf about two-thirds of the way down the stem.

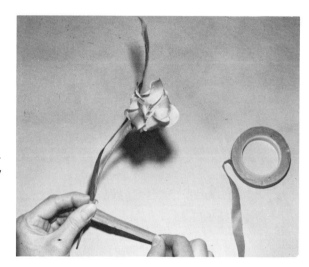

Day Lily

The suggested colors for day lilies are: pale yellow, bright yellow, orange, and deep rust for the petals and green for the leaves.

Using the day lily pattern in Illus. 82, cut out six petals and

Illus. 81. You do not need a green thumb to "grow" beautiful day lilies like these—just some silk, some glue and some wire!

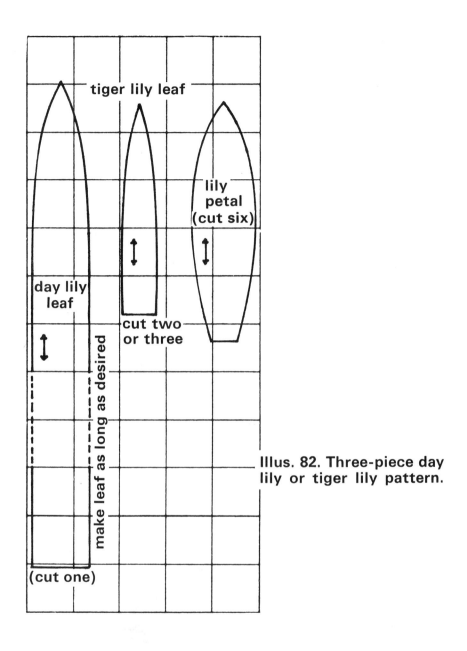

tiger lily leaf

lily petal (cut six)

day lily leaf

make leaf as long as desired

cut two or three

(cut one)

Illus. 82. Three-piece day lily or tiger lily pattern.

one leaf for each flower. Roll the edges of the petals and leaf. Shade the petals with soft pastels if desired, copying a clear color picture of the day lily or following the close-up in Illus. 83. Pale orange silk was used to make the petals. A yellow pastel stick was applied to the base of each petal and a bright orange pastel stick was used above the yellow for shading. The orange was blended towards the top of each petal. You can use a brown pastel stick to deepen the orange color.

After you have shaded the petals, continue making the flower parts as follows: Cut seven pieces of white cotton-covered wire, each about 5 inches (125 mm.) long, for six stamens and one pistil. Make the stamens larger than usual. Stick the stamens in plastic foam to dry.

Using a felt-tip marker, color the filaments (stems) yellow or orange and the anthers (heads) deep yellow, orange, or brown. Color the remaining wire yellow or orange to serve as the pistil.

Cut six petal supports and color them to match the petals. Glue a supporting wire to the middle of the back of each petal. Stick the petals in plastic foam to dry.

Cut one piece of heavy green cotton-covered wire (the length of the leaf plus 2 inches or 50 mm.) for the leaf support. Glue to the middle of the back of the leaf. Stick the leaf in plastic foam to dry.

Before assembling the day lily, take each of the petals and place them right side up on the work surface. Rub the yellow pastel stick down the middle of each petal, over the support wire. This completes the shading of the petals.

Assembling the Day Lily

Begin assembling the day lily with the six stamens and pistil. The tops of the stamens should be even. The pistil should protrude from the middle of the stamens and extend about an inch (25 mm.) higher than the stamens. Hold the stamens and the pistil together with a short piece of floral tape, attached about 3 inches (75 mm.) down from the top of the stamens.

Apply a small amount of glue across the bottom of each petal. Space three petals evenly round the stamens. The glue holds the petals in place. The stamens should extend about 3 inches (75 mm.) above the base of the petals. Place

Illus. 83. Close-up of the day lily. Follow this for the shading.

the remaining three petals around and between the first three petals. Always keep the bottoms of the petals even.

Cut the extending wire supports different lengths to eliminate bulk. Attach a stem wire to the extending wire supports with floral tape. Wrap the floral tape down the stem. Attach the leaf about two-thirds of the way down with additional tape.

Shape the day lily by flaring the upper part of each petal outwards. Spray the finished flower with a clear acrylic spray or fixative to set the shading.

Tiger Lily

Make the tiger lily by following the directions for the day lily on pages 49 to 52, but with these changes: Use a fine-line felt-tip marker or charcoal pencil to make dots on the petals as shown in Illus. 85. Concentrate the dots near the middle of each petal. Cut the wires for the stamens and pistil 6 inches (150 mm.) long. Enlarge one end of the wire for the pistil in the same way you would make a small stamen.

The pistil should extend an inch (25 mm.) higher than the stamens and 4½ inches (112.5 mm.) above the base of the

Illus. 84. Even you will think your silk tiger lilies are real, if they look like the ones shown here!

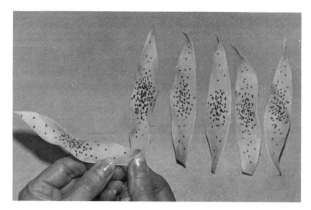

Illus. 85. Make dots with a fine-line felt-tip marker or charcoal pencil as shown here.

Illus. 86. Twist the stamens' anthers perpendicularly to their filaments.

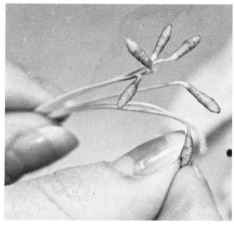

Illus. 87. Shape the tiger lily by curling the petals away from the stamens.

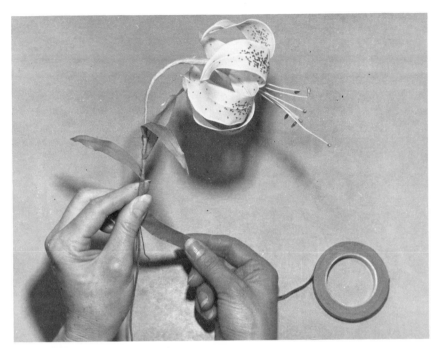

Illus. 88. Attach several short, narrow leaves to the stem, beginning about 4 inches below the flower.

petals. Twist the stamens' anthers (heads) perpendicularly to their filaments (stems) (Illus. 86).

Shape the tiger lily by curling the petals away from the stamens (Illus. 87). Bend the neck of the stem so the flower is facing downward. Then attach several short, narrow leaves to the stem, beginning about 4 inches (100 mm.) below the flower (Illus. 88).

You may attach two or three flowers to one stem if desired.

Bearded Iris

Illus. 89. If you love bearded irises, here is your chance to make some yourself. A beautiful arrangement of them will cheer you up all year round.

The suggested colors for bearded irises are: lavender, purple, yellow, and white for the petals and green for the leaves.

Using the iris pattern in Illus. 90, cut out six large petals, three small petals, and one leaf for each flower.

Roll the edges of the petals and the leaf. Set aside. Cut nine pieces of white cotton-covered wire, each about 5 inches (125 mm.) long, for petal supports. Using a felt-tip marker, color the wires to match the petals. Using full-strength glue sparingly, glue a supporting wire to the middle of the back of each petal. Stick the petals in plastic foam to dry.

Cut a piece of heavy green cotton-covered wire (the length of the leaf plus 2 inches or 50 mm.) for the leaf support. Glue the supporting wire to the middle of the back of the leaf. Stick the leaf in plastic foam to dry.

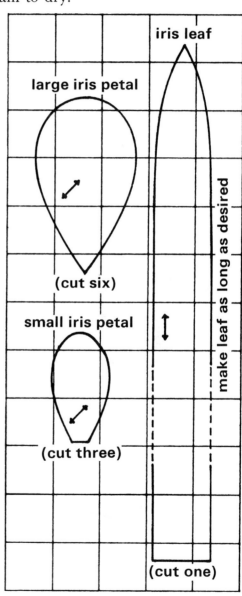

Illus. 90. Three-piece bearded iris pattern.

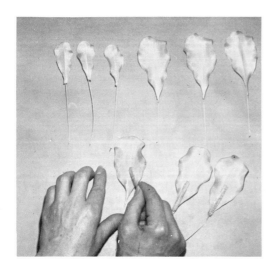

Illus. 91. Glue a piece of chenille trim to the middle of each large iris petal.

Next, make three small stamens and stick in plastic foam to dry. Using a felt-tip marker, color the stamens yellow.

Cut three pieces of yellow chenille stem, each $1\frac{1}{4}$ inches (31 mm.) long. (You can purchase chenille stems in various colors at craft shops. Chenille is a tufted, velvety cord used for trimming.) Use the chenille to trim three of the large petals. Glue the trim to the middle of each petal, even with the bottom (Illus. 91).

Assembling the Bearded Iris

Begin assembling the bearded iris by placing the three small petals together in a triangular position. Hold the small petals in place with a short piece of floral tape wrapped below the petals. These petals curve outwards, so be sure the support wires are underneath. Place one small stamen under each of the small petals. The stamens should extend about an inch (25 mm.) above the base of the petals. Hold the stamens in place with a short piece of floral tape (Illus. 92).

Add the three large plain petals around and between the small petals. Hold these petals in place with tape. These petals curve upwards, so be sure the right sides of the petals are facing outwards (Illus. 93).

Add the three remaining large petals (with chenille trim) by

58

Illus. 92. Place the three small petals together and then add one small stamen under each of these petals. Hold in place with floral tape.

placing one between each of the large petals already in place. These petals curve downwards directly under each of the small petals (Illus. 94). Hold them in place with tape. Always keep the bottoms of the petals even.

Cut the extending wire supports different lengths to eliminate bulk. Attach a stem wire to the extending wire supports with floral tape. Wrap the tape down the stem. Then attach the leaf about two-thirds of the way down with additional tape (Illus. 95).

Illus. 93. Add the three large, plain petals around and between the small ones.

Illus. 94. Add the three chenille-trimmed petals between each of the large petals already in place.

59

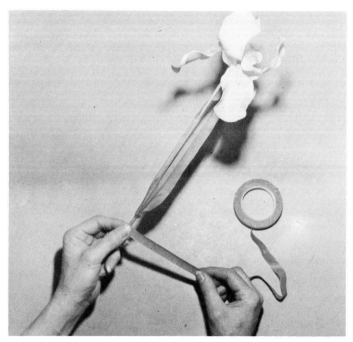

Illus. 95. Wrap the stem with floral tape, adding the leaf about two-thirds of the way down.

Shape the iris by curving three of the large petals upwards and the other three (with chenille trim) downwards. The stamens are hidden under the small petals that curve outwards and above the chenille-trimmed petals.

Sweet Pea

The suggested colors for sweet peas are: white, blue, pink, deep pink, and lavender for the petals.

Using the sweet pea pattern in Illus. 96, cut out six petal pieces. This makes three flowers for each stem.

Illus. 96. One-piece sweet pea pattern.

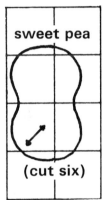

sweet pea

(cut six)

Illus. 97. This strikingly elegant flower arrangement is simply a collection of silk sweet peas.

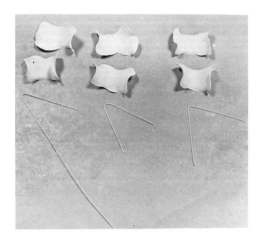

Roll the edges of the petals and set aside. Cut one piece of white cotton-covered wire about 10 inches (250 mm.) long. Cut two more pieces of white about 4 inches (100 mm.) long. Using a felt-tip marker, color the wires to match the petals.

Cut two pieces of small green cotton-covered wire, about 4 inches (100 mm.) long, for tendrils. Wrap the green wires round a pencil to form coils.

Assembling the Sweet Pea

Two of the petal pieces you have cut and rolled form one flower. Bend each of the wires about 2 inches (50 mm.) from one

Illus. 99. Place two of the petal pieces together, loop the bend in the wires around each group, gather the petal pieces upwards, and twist the wire round the middle.

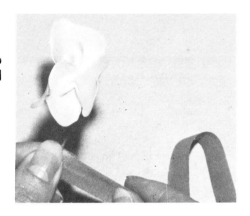

Illus. 100. Wrap the two short stems with floral tape.

end (Illus. 98). Place two of the petal pieces together (rolled sides up), and loop around the bend in one of the wires. Gather the petal pieces upwards and twist the wire round the middle to hold in place (Illus. 99). Follow this procedure to make the remaining two flowers.

Wrap the two short flower stems with floral tape (Illus. 100). Wrap the long stem with tape, attaching one of the short stems about 2 inches (50 mm.) down and the other 2 inches (50 mm.) lower. Attach the coiled tendrils at random (Illus. 101).

Illus. 101. Wrap the long stem with floral tape, adding the short stems where shown. Attach the coiled tendrils at random.

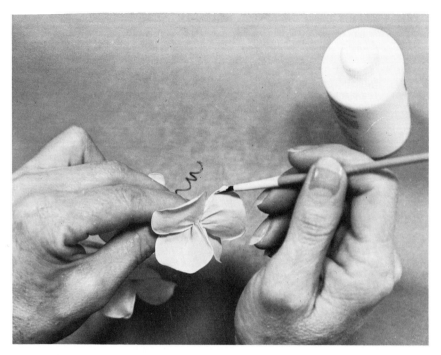

Illus. 102. Pull two of the petals upwards in a fan shape. Then glue them together.

Shape the flowers by pulling two of the petals upwards and in a fan shape. Glue these two pieces together (Illus. 102). The other two petals protrude forwards. Glue these two pieces together across the top.

You may add a heavier stem wire for a stronger stem. Overlap the flower stem and a stem wire, and wrap together with floral tape.

Rose and Bud

The suggested colors for roses are: white, pink, yellow, orange, and red for the petals and green for the leaves.

Make the rose pattern according to Illus. 104 for a large rose. For a smaller rose, decrease the size of the petals. One small and one large rose were used in the arrangement shown in Illus. 103. The bud was made by decreasing the size of the small petals.

Illus. 103. An awesome, undying arrangement of roses is a gift which will never be forgotten.

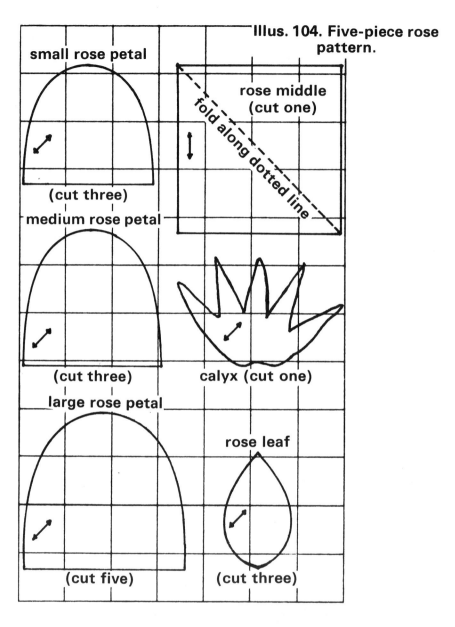

Illus. 104. Five-piece rose pattern.

small rose petal

rose middle (cut one)

fold along dotted line

(cut three)

medium rose petal

(cut three)

calyx (cut one)

large rose petal

rose leaf

(cut five)

(cut three)

Using the rose pattern in Illus. 104, cut out one square for the middle, three small petals, three medium petals, five large petals, and one calyx for each rose. Cut out one square, three small petals, and one calyx for each bud. Cut out three leaves for each rose.

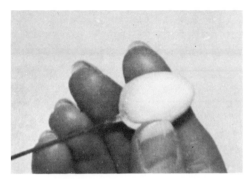

Illus. 105. Make a small closed loop on the end of a stem wire.

Illus. 106. Form the middle of the rose by glueing a cotton ball around the wire loop in an oval shape.

Make a small closed loop on one end of a stem wire (Illus. 105). Form the middle of the rose by glueing a cotton ball around the loop in an oval shape (Illus. 106). Stick in plastic foam to dry.

Fold the square of silk into a triangular shape. Have the fold of the triangle at the top. Place the oval inside the middle of the triangle (Illus. 107). Fold the sides in and around the oval. Pinch the raw edges round the stem and hold in place

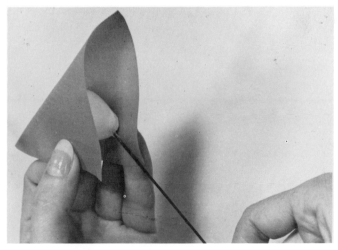

Illus. 107. Place the cotton oval inside the middle of the triangle you form.

with spool wire wound round the bottom of the oval (Illus. 108). Clip away any excess silk below the wire.

Next, finish the rounded edges of the petals and set aside. Finish the edges of the leaves. Cut three pieces of small green cotton-covered wire, each about 5 inches (125 mm.) long, for leaf supports. Glue a supporting wire to the middle of the back of each leaf. Stick the leaves in plastic foam to dry.

Assembling the Rose, Bud, and Leaves

To assemble the rose, begin with the three small petals. Apply glue across the inside bottom raw edge of one of the small petals. The roll of the petal should be on the outside. Wrap the small petal loosely round the heart of the rose, pinch-

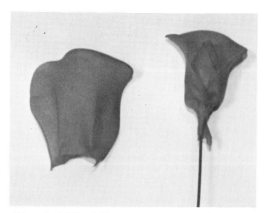

Illus. 110. Add the other two small petals, forming a box pleat as shown in Illus. 109.

Illus. 109. Wrap the small petal loosely round the heart of the rose, pinching the base as shown.

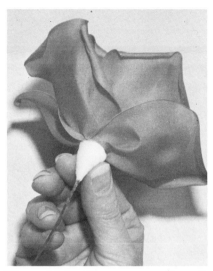

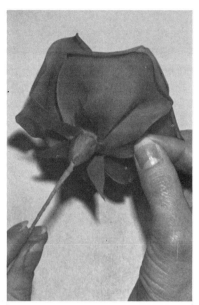

Illus. 111. Glue a small roll of cotton round the bottom of the rose as a base for the calyx.

Illus. 112. Glue the calyx round the cotton base.

ing the base of the petal round the stem wire (Illus. 109, right).

Apply glue across the bottom of the remaining two small petals. Take up about half of the width of the bottom edge of each of these petals by forming a box pleat (Illus. 109, left and Illus. 110). Form the box pleat on the outside of the petal. Attach the two small petals to either side of the first petal. If necessary, hold the petals in place with a short piece of spool wire wound round the base of the petals.

Apply glue to the bottom edges of the three medium petals, form box pleats as before, and attach these petals evenly around the small petals, gathering them in slightly. Hold in place with wire. Apply glue to the bottom edges of the five large petals, form box pleats, and attach these petals evenly around the medium petals, gathering in slightly. Hold in place with wire. Keep the base of the petals even with the bottom of the oval middle.

Glue a small roll of cotton round the bottom of the rose as a base for the calyx (Illus. 111). Glue the calyx round the cotton base (Illus. 112).

Make the bud in the same way as the whole rose, but using the three small petals only. Wrap floral tape down the stem.

Place the three rose leaves together with one leaf extending about an inch (25 mm.) higher than the other two. Wrap the stems together with floral tape, beginning about an inch (25 mm.) below the bottom leaves. Spread these two leaves outwards.

Wrap floral tape down the stem, attaching the leaves as desired with additional floral tape. You may use the rose bud singly or attach it to the stem of the rose.

To shape the rose and bud, roll the petals' edges outwards and under (Illus. 113).

Illus. 113. To shape the rose, roll the petals' edges outwards and under.

Making Medium- or Large-Petalled Flowers

You can easily make flowers other than those already described by copying real flowers. Select medium or large flowers that have only a few petals. You need two of the actual flowers to work with: one which you will tear apart to make a pattern and the other to copy while assembling the flower.

Petals, Leaves and Calyx

Carefully remove the calyx from one of the flowers. Flatten it out, lay it on a piece of cardboard, and draw around it.

Next, look at the way the petals are positioned. The petals may all be the same size, or they may be different sizes. Place one of each size petal on a piece of cardboard. Draw round the petals, adding an allowance for finishing the edges.

Follow the same procedure for the leaves. If the leaves have jagged edges, you do not need an allowance. Cut out the cardboard patterns and label with all necessary information.

To determine how to place the pattern on the silk, draw a horizontal line through the longest part of the pattern. Draw a perpendicular line through the horizontal line. Then draw a 45-degree (diagonal) line through the crossed lines. (It makes no difference in which direction you draw the diagonal line.) If the pattern is elongated, as is the case with the day lily, then use the horizontal line for placement of the pattern. If the petal is more rounded, then use the diagonal line. Place the correct line parallel to the selvage of the fabric.

Illus. 114. Draw a horizontal, a perpendicular and a diagonal line as shown to determine how to place your pattern on the silk.

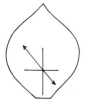

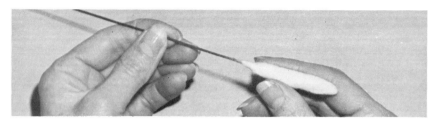

Illus. 115. To make a center for an arum lily, glue a thick layer of cotton round the top of a stem wire, covering about 2 inches of the wire.

Flower Middles

Now study the middle of the flower. Duplicate the middle, as nearly as possible, by using one of the methods previously shown in this book, or by adopting other ideas. For example, a piece of straight chenille stem, cut the appropriate length, could serve as the middle of an althea. You could produce a realistic middle for an arum lily by glueing a thick layer of absorbent cotton round the top of a stem wire, covering about 2 inches (50 mm.) of the wire (Illus. 115). When dry, color the cotton yellow with a felt-tip marker.

To make a daisy-type middle, coil a piece of chenille stem the desired size. Bend the remaining end of the chenille stem to the middle of the bottom side of the coil and then bend the wire downwards. Cut the extending chenille stem 2 inches (50 mm.) long. Clip the chenille off the extending wire (Illus. 116).

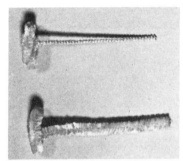

Illus. 116. For a daisy-like middle make a chenille coil and bend the wire downwards.

Illus. 117. Make a different middle by covering a round button with velveteen, as shown.

Illus. 118. The daisy in the middle of this arrangement has a coiled chenille center.

You can make the same type of middle by covering a rounded button with a small scrap of velveteen or other material (Illus. 117). Cut the velveteen into a circle large enough to cover the rounded button. With a needle and thread, run a gathering stitch around the outer edge of the circle of fabric. Apply glue to the bottom of the button. Place the fabric over the button and pull the gathering stitch tightly round the underside of the button, smoothing the fabric over the top. The gathering stitch and the glue should hold the fabric firmly

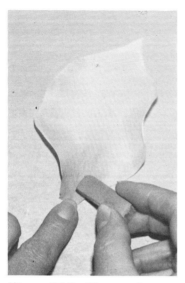

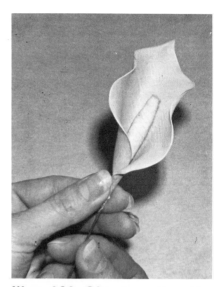

Illus. 119. To make an arum lily, shade both sides of the lower part of the spathe.

Illus. 120. Glue together the lower ½ inch of the two sides of the spathe so that they meet at the front.

in place. Glue the covered button to the middle of the flower after you have assembled the petals.

Assembling the Flowers

After you have made the pattern, and gathered the supplies, you are ready to make the flower. Study the real flower carefully. Observe the coloring and shading, the flow of the petals, the placement of the leaves, and the curve of the stem. If you follow the general instructions for construction, your flowers should turn out quite well.

To clarify the procedure, the arum lily is used as an example. Gently pull the large spathe (actually a large bract) away from the spatix (the spike in the middle of the flower). Flatten out the spathe on a piece of cardboard and carefully draw around it. Remove the spathe and enlarge the pattern by adding ⅛ inch (3.18 mm.) around the outer edge. Label the pattern with all necessary information, then cut out the cardboard pattern.

Make the spike of the lily, using the method described on page 72. Trace the pattern onto white silk that has been properly sized. Cut out the silk spathe and finish the edges. Notice the subtle green coloring at the base of the real spathe. Shade the silk spathe with a light green pastel following the directions given under *Shading the Petals* on page 16. In this instance, however, shade both sides of the lower part of the spathe (Illus. 119).

The arum lily does not require a support wire, so proceed by applying a small amount of glue on the inside bottom of the spathe. Glue the spathe around the bottom of the spike so that the spike extends about 2 inches (50 mm.) above the bottom of the spathe. Glue together the lower $\frac{1}{2}$ inch (12.5 mm.) of the two sides meeting at the front (Illus. 120).

Wrap the stem wire with floral tape, adding leaves if desired. Shape the flower by curling the edges outwards (Illus. 121).

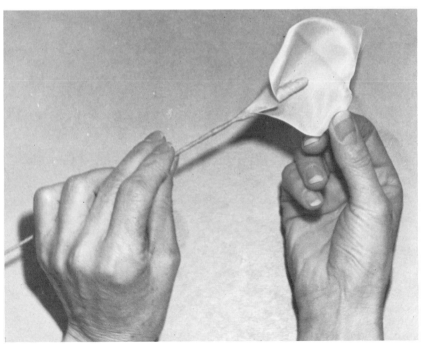

Illus. 121. Shape the flower by curling the edges of the petals outwards.

Increasing the Varieties of Flowers

Daisy-type middles are easy enough to make, but unless you make a large daisy like the gloriosa, the small petals are very difficult to roll. Then too, a flower with numerous petals is very time consuming to create. The following instructions should help to add to the kinds of flowers that you can create on your own.

First, you need a piece of foam rubber, a half inch (12.5 mm.) thick, or several layers of art foam. (You can purchase art foam at most craft shops.) Cut the art foam into four pieces, each measuring 8 × 12 inches (20 × 30 cm.). Place the pieces together and wrap a cotton fabric around the foam. Tack the cotton covering in place.

Decide on the flower you want to make and have two of the actual flowers on hand. Select a fabric that is suitable for the flower. You can use any kind of fabric with this method because

Illus. 122. To form the edges of petals which are really too small to roll, moisten the petals and place them on a foam pad. With a heated teaspoon or knife, apply pressure as shown.

**Illus. 123. Dried plant material combines beauti-
fully with silk flowers to form a unique, permanent flower arrangement.**

you do not roll the edges of the petals. Size the fabric properly
before you cut out the petals and leaves.

Look closely at the curves of the petals. For example, some
petals are quite rounded at the bottom, curving outwards at
the top. To form such a petal, proceed by moistening one of
the fabric petals with a damp cloth. Place the moistened petal
on the foam pad, right side next to the pad. Using a heated
teaspoon, apply pressure to the lower half of the petal. Turn the

petal over and lightly move the end of the hot teaspoon around the edge of the petal. Form each of the petals in the same way. You can also mould leaves in much the same manner. Use the tines of a fork or the edge of a dull knife to form the veining of leaves. Experiment with this procedure until you have achieved the desired effects.

Often, it is not necessary to glue the supporting wires to the backs of the petals. Attach the stem wire to the middle of the flower. Then apply glue to the inside base of the petals and glue to the sides or underside of the middle. If a calyx is necessary, use an adaptation of the directions given under the instructions for the rose on page 69.

Coloring the Fabric

Since it is possible to use fabrics other than China silk to make flowers, you might wish to experiment with the coloring of the fabric. You can use fabric dyes to obtain colors not otherwise available. Follow the general directions for mixing the purchased dyes. Pour a little of each color to be used into small bowls. Moisten the prepared petals with water to which a little detergent has been added and then dip them in the desired color. Place the petals on absorbent paper towels and blot with additional towels. If the petal fabric is heavy, paint the dye on with a small brush.

China silk is the traditional material for making the flowers in this book. Less expensive silk and rayon blends, however, are a satisfactory alternative. If you are unable to purchase China silk locally, write to the following:

Rietta's Fabrics, Inc.	Joanne's Fine Fabrics	S. Beckenstein, Inc.
222 Greensprings Highway	105 First Avenue S.E.	130 Orchard Street
Greensprings Shopping Center	Cedar Rapids, Iowa 52401	New York, New York 10002
Birmingham, Alabama 35209		
Col. G.D. Morgan	Gift Barrell	Genie Fabrics
393 Main Street	603-1/2 Metairie Road	3758 Summer Ave.
Los Altos, California 94022	Metairie, Louisiana 70005	Memphis, Tennessee 38122
Brenda's Fabric	Eunice Farmer Fabrics, Inc.	Southern Fabrics
4700 N. University	9814 Clayton Road	1210 Galleria Mall
Peoria, Illinois 61614	St. Louis, Missouri 53124	Houston, Texas 77056

Flower Arrangements

You should consider several things before making flowers for an arrangement. First, decide where the arrangement will be placed. This determines the size of the arrangement and the various colors of the flowers. Select the varieties of flowers and colors to harmonize with the surrounding area. Choose a suitable container for the flowers. Have a clear mental picture of how you want the arrangement to look. Then estimate the number of flowers required. You can make extra leaves to use as fillers in an arrangement. You can also use dried plant materials which combine beautifully with silk flowers, as you can see in Illus. 123.

Assembly-Line Method

It is easier to make all of one kind of flower before proceeding to another. If you do this, an assembly-line method of making the flowers can be established. As an example, suppose you need three day lilies for an arrangement. Begin by cutting out 18 petals and three leaves. Color the petals, if necessary, and roll the edges of the petals and leaves. Next, shade all the petals if desired. Attach all supporting wires at one time. Make 18 stamens and three pistils. Color all stamens and pistils. Finally, assemble each lily.

Conclusion

Nature is constantly changing, with something new to be discovered each time you observe it. A pursuit of such new discoveries can also enhance any form of art you strive to master. Making silk flowers can, in this way, be as unlimited as you choose to make it. Hopefully, you have been inspired to continue expanding your creativeness in making silk flowers.

Index